SAVED SINGLE AND SATISFIED

Developing Into the Woman of God with Purpose

Lisa Moore-Banks

Saved Single And Satisfied
Lisa Moore-Banks

Published by:
Anointed Words Publishing Co.

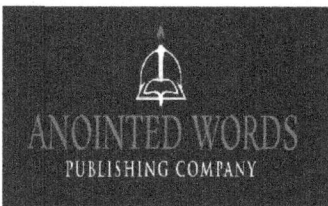

 Address all inquiries to:
2344 Shawnee Rd., #109
Lima, OH 45805
Email: awpubco@gmail.com
www.awpubco.com

ISBN: 978-09977397-5-6
Printed in the United States of America

Contents

FOREWORD

It gives me great honor to acknowledge the writer of this inspiring book, "Saved, Single and Satisfied," by Lisa Moore – Banks.

Lord knows, I would have avoided many troubles, experiences, and heartaches if I had been fortunate to have had my hands on a copy of this book!

There were so many times in my life as a single woman where I did not know what to do or how to do it. The 12 Steps in this book is the kind of material that arms you with knowledge and empowers you with the word of God to help you navigate through some of the tough challenges in life.

I'm encouraged by the insight and real talk of life experiences that will help provide single women guidance while trying to live godly lives. This book, I believe, is the answer to some of your struggles!

Ladies get ready to dive into this incredible 12-step handbook for Christian women designed to help you become the woman of God you were purposed to be!

It's been my blessing to watch this amazing,

beautiful woman grow, mature, press, share her gift with the world and become all God has purposed her to be!

Love you, the best is yet to come!

Pastor Kim Lyons,
In Faith Ministries International

DEDICATION

God has given me four amazing sons; Christian, Michael, Adam and Ryan. Thank you for your love, understanding and patience. I love you so much, with all of my heart.

God has brought us through and has been so good to our family. We are blessed and highly favored by God.

Mom.

Lisa Moore-Banks

INTRODUCTION

To God Be The Glory!

Greetings, great and mighty women of God, in the Name of our Lord and Savior Jesus Christ.

For us, single women, to talk about our problems and issues with finance, sex and our spiritual walk with Christ can be stressful. Most churches don't have single programs in which we can spend time in a private, trusting atmosphere having a Q & A meeting. Being single, the subject of sex can be taboo in the church and you will be, or at least feel like, you're deemed a sinner for just the thought of sex. Our finances can also be troubling at times and how we spend our money will have our hands tied behind our backs, leaving us in financial lack or poverty. None of this should happen to a saved, Christian single woman.

God has given me this handbook because I have already gone through and was delivered from the struggle of sexual addiction, financial woes, and low self-esteem. I began to walk in my gifts and calling for my purpose in the Kingdom of God by learning how to be consistent and develop a personal relationship with God. Staying focused on my purpose for the Kingdom Of God and realizing that none of my problems and issues were really about me, helped me to give God praise through my struggles and difficulties in life as a woman of God.

I want you to know you are not alone in your journey with God. If you felt that you were, you're not alone anymore! You now have a voice and an ambassador for Jesus Christ. God has given me instructions on how to deal with this sensitive topic on sex and the demons that control us during the late night hours. We, as single women, can learn to love ourselves and be satisfied with knowing God loves us more.

Living saved and single really doesn't have to be hard or difficult. You can actually have it all and then some; that's scripture. You are destined with a purposed to serve in the Kingdom of God, free from struggles and sins. This guide will help you to learn to love yourself and give you self-confidence in knowing that you will be just fine.

Lisa Moore-Banks

I pray that after going through the 12-Steps, you can literally birth out your calling and know that you are purposed for the Kingdom of God. You will be able to learn to develop a love for Jesus Christ and have a much deeper relationship with God, and living life as a *SAVED, SINGLE AND SATISFIED* woman of God until God says otherwise.

~Be Blessed. Be Encouraged.

A TRUE WOMAN OF GOD
You Are a Warrior Woman of God

This book is dedicated to my beloved grandmother, a great woman of God, the late Mother, Hattie Mae Bell-Moore. To all my single sisters in the ministry of "Girl Talk" and my mentor, a beautiful woman of God, Minister, Dr. Leah McCray, author, attorney, and leader of Girl Talk.

Who can find a virtuous woman? For her price is far above rubies. Proverbs 31:10.

Lisa Moore-Banks

Step 1 - Respect Your Temple.

I Corinthians 6:19 (KJV)
~What? Know ye not that you're body is the temple of the Holy Ghost which is in you, which ye have of God, and ye are not your own?

When giving your life to Jesus Christ, we entered into a covenant, an agreement, promising to obey and follow his commandments from the word of God. Our life is not our own. God created us. Therefore, he has ownership of the blueprints of our mind, body, and soul. Although He gives us free will, we cannot just treat our body any old kind of way. From the crown of our head to the soles of our feet, we are to live holy and acceptable in the sight of God. We must always be holy from the inside out. How you carry yourselves reflect who you are in Christ.

Question? If former President and First Lady Obama invited you to the White House for a night of elegance, would you wear a revealing dress with the neckline so low that your "girls" (breast) are hanging out? No, you would wear your best, so how come your best is not good enough for the Most High God, the King of Kings, Jesus Christ? Although we are single, we are married to Jesus Christ. Think about it; if you were married, do you really think a man of God would want his wife at church, or anywhere else, with her "girls' (breast) and butt hanging out for all the world to see? I doubt that he would.

We are to look our best and still have some class by not showing our "you know what." In reality, every man that comes to church is not saved and, yes, of course, he should not be looking, but sister you put it all out there for the world to see. Don't have your skirt so short that you can't even kneel down at the altar. Yes, we are to come to church just as we are, to a point. The meaning of "come as you are" refers to the newcomers to Christ. After you have been on your journey with God, there comes a time when you must learn to stand out from the sinners, the unbelievers in this world. We are to be identified as Christians, the true believers of God.

You may be wondering why I'm breaking it down like this, but you would be surprised how many women, especially from the ages of 18-25, don't understand and come to Sunday morning worship as if they're going to the Saturday night local club, this is not acceptable. Separate yourself from the world, baby girl. You are royalty and joint-heir with Jesus Christ who sits on the throne.

Are you on a budget that won't allow you to buy new clothing? Later, in the handbook, I will discuss how to gain in your finances, but there are ways to keep your closet fresh and new. I love second-hand stores, consignment boutiques and Goodwill. Especially if you live in a larger city, you will have more variety, and you can find just about anything and everything. The wealthy people take their things there or have garage sales. So be open-minded and learn to save a buck. Until then, keep what you do have clean, even if you have to wash it out by hand and just come anyhow, no matter what you have in your closet. Remember modesty is the best policy.

Women of God should look classy, that doesn't mean that you have to buy a $200-$500 suit. I try to model myself after my Co-Pastor, Kim Lyons, who is very beautiful and elegant with a whole lot of class. Even when she is just wearing jeans or casual wear, you never see her showing off her cleavage or having a slit up to her thighs or a mini skirt. So find someone with similar taste and style that you like, who can be an example of who God wants you to be and take note and learn how to be and look like the woman of God that your Creator intended for you to be. Respect yourself always.

Do you know the best way to scare off a man? Your mouth. As Christian women, we should always conduct ourselves as ladies when speaking. The one thing I cannot stand to hear is a woman curse like a sailor and, of course, we should not be swearing or cursing at others. Also, we should not be loud and obnoxious using the same language of the world. The drama, always overreacting to the situation before they become situations. As soon as something minor happens, you're all in an uproar only to find out it's nothing. Calm down, relax and say a prayer first. I use to have a potty mouth, but God delivered me and set me free. I use to argue just for attention, and this was not lady like at all.

Being women of God who are standing on his word, we should not be engaging in any sinful activity; this is a violation against your body which is the temple of the Holy Ghost. The Holy Spirit cannot and will not dwell in an unclean temple. Most people refer to this as sexual, but what you do to your body that's not of God is sinful. If your home is a hot mess, dirty and covered in filth, would you expect to have a special guest of valor stay with you? Do you really think the Queen of England would stay in your unclean home? So, God, our Father, the Most High God will not dwell in our home of filth. So be mindful of what can contaminate your spirit man and affect your temple which houses the spirit of God and The Holy Ghost.

Philippians 4:8 *"Finally my brethren, whatsoever things are true, whatsoever things are honest, whatsoever things are just, whatsoever things are* *pure, whatsoever things that are lovely and of good report; if there be any virtue and if there be any praise think on these things.*

SUMMARY

God loves us for who we are. However, he expect us, as women, to look the part and live the part of being a good, godly woman. This does not mean that we can't have an eye for fashion, it's simply saying, have enough love and respect for yourself not to flash everyone with skin and breast. Be mindful of your selection of clothing when attending church. Know the importance of body maintenance and proper hygiene. If you smell good and look good, you feel good! Most of all keep your temple clean from sin so that the Holy Spirit may dwell within you always.

Lisa Moore-Banks

"A CLASS ACT TO FOLLOW" CO-PASTOR KIM LYONS

"Where you are in life right at this moment does not determine your future."
~Pastor Prophetess Author Kim Lyons

www.kimlyonsministries.com
Co-Pastor of In Faith Ministries International Lima, OH 45804

I am very blessed to be sitting under the leadership of Co-Pastor, Kim Lyons. As an anointed woman of God, her beauty of Jesus Christ illuminates from the inside out. She's confident in knowing she's a child of God. She speaks with such great force of power and authority over every devil and demons; her favorite line is "quit being a scary cat."

She encourages both men and women to stand up and be bold, confident and courageous in their walk with Christ. Pastor Kim has inspired many women in their walk and journey with God. With her business like mind and love in her heart for God's people, she takes her duties as Pastor very seriously, realizing it was never about her but always about God. She inspired me and encouraged me always and would say "LiLi, just trust God. He's faithful and be consistent."

I would not be who I am today as a woman of God, a mother, daughter and now, author. I love you, Pastor Kim. Thank You!

Worksheet #1

My life as a living sacrifice.

List 5 things you can do to keep your mind and body a living sacrifice:

1._____

2._____

3._____

4._____

5._____

PRAYER

Father, God, in the name of Jesus Christ, I pray that I continue to keep my heart, mind, and body on you at all times. When things get uncomfortable, I find comfort and peace in knowing you are our refuge and keeper of my soul and you will give me rest and satisfaction in your love. Amen.

Step 2 - Love Who You Are In Christ.

1 Corinthians 13:4-7 (KJV)
"Love suffers long and is kind; love does not envy, love does not parade itself, is not puffed up; does not behave rudely, does not seek its own, is not provoked thinks no evil does not rejoice in iniquity, but rejoices in the truth; bears all things believes all things endures all things.

Single women of God, you must love who you are in Christ. God did not make any mistakes when creating you and designing the blueprint of your life. Although we admire other strong, powerful women of God who preach and teach with a heavy anointing, don't get to the point where you are looking at them wishing you were moving in your purpose with their power. You have no clue what it took for them to get where they needed to be for others to admire them. They too had to go through the process to get to their purpose in the Kingdom of God. They had their share of struggles, headaches, and heartache, all while walking in the valley of the shadow of death. God had to mold and shape them and put them in the fiery furnace for purification just like he's doing you. What God has for you is for you, and what God has for them is for them. Enjoy and love who you are right now in Christ, its all for a purpose, a perfect plan that God has just for you.

So what does real love mean to you? Women are emotional creatures, for most, love is simply an emotional matter of the heart, so you think? We easily become heartbroken when it comes to love. Love should never hurt. Love is kind, gentle and giving. The first love of your life should be God, he loved you before the world was created and he knew all about you.

Then there's the love of family and friends. As you become older, you will learn what it's all about to fall in love. However, there are 3-types of love, and as singles who desire to be loved, we must know the difference between them to avoid future headaches which come from a lack of understanding in this area.

Use discernment when meeting and dating men, not all men who claim to be saved are; they, too, are looking to be married, but maybe for the wrong reasons, or not on the same level of faith and anointing that you are. Do not be unequally yoked.

There are three Kinds of Love:

Eros Love   Agape Love   Philos Love

Eros Love

Falling in love with the opposite sex based on feelings. The matters of the heart that causes emotional attachment.

Agape Love

The divine love of God that commands us to love all humanity. This kind of love does not involve emotional attachment; it's a requirement.

Philos Love

The love you have the moment you lay your eyes on your parents. This love can attach itself to the heart, and you can be disappointed and hurt. It comes with great expectation from the person on whom you most depend.

Love can be complicated because, for the world and unbelievers, it's an emotion, a matter of the heart. But the love of God is the agape love that never deals with emotions or feelings because, God, himself is Love. He's so much greater and deeper than the heart. The one way you can eliminate all the fuss and worries that come from not being in a relationship and having a man's love is to first fall in love with God. As women, we should never depend on any one person to love us other than God, and it's a fact that he does. Depending on anyone to make you happy is only going to result in making yourself miserable, because you have not learned to love yourself.

Do not confuse sex with love; it actually has nothing to do with love as they are two different things entirely. Sexual activity will be discussed later in the handbook, but let me now say that wanting to love in order to have sex, and having sex, in order to be in love, are both results of lust for one or the other. Just because you're practicing celibacy does not mean you're loveless.

God's love is a miraculous love. God is the only one who loved you before you came into existence in this world, before you were even conceived in your mother's womb. Your parents can not love you before conception, how can any person love someone before knowing who they are? How could Jesus Christ die on the cross without love? That in itself was the power of God's love. *John 3:16 "For God so loved the world that he gave his only begotten son that whosoever believe in him shall not perish but have everlasting life."*

Worksheet #2

You are fearfully and wonderfully made. Ps 139:14

Find 10 things you love about yourself and possess it.

1._____

2._____

3._____

4._____

5._____

6._____

7._____

8._____

9._____

10._____

I will praise thee, For I AM wonderfully and fearfully made marvelous are thy works, and my soul knoweth right well. Psalms 139:14

SUMMARY

Praise God for who you are right now and where you are heading in the future. Continue to allow him to work on you, although none of us are perfect, we all can strive for excellence. God created you to be you and you were made in his image. You are made perfect in his sight. God cannot make any mistakes. Love yourself and make time for you. Know that you are one of a kind, uniquely made and there is only one you and that makes you a very special woman of God.

PRAYER

Father, God, in the name of Jesus, I come boldly to the throne asking for you to help me walk in love at all times. Lord, help me to understand the importance of agape love. Please help me to learn how to wait on eros love and help me to philos love my family and friends. Lord teach me how to love myself and others the way that you love me. Amen.

Step 3 - Possess the Power and the Image Of God.

Philippians 4:13 (KJV)

I can do all things through Christ which strengthens me.

As single women, it's very important to keep ourselves busy doing positive things for the Lord. Find a ministry you can be a part of or work in the community helping others. Spread your wings and step outside of the box of your comfort zone by doing things you normally wouldn't do. Expand your spiritual horizon and get creative. Develop new ideas and projects for work, school or church. Take up a hobby; the one thing you have always wanted to do. Take up the piano or take an art class. Get involved with community events and programs to help women in need or children by going to a shelter to volunteer.

Educate yourself by taking a class at your local college.

Well, you're probably thinking, I can't do this, or you're not motivated enough. Well, who is the most creative one of all time? Your Father, GOD; he created the world and painted it with beautiful blue skies, white clouds, and green grass. God created the oceans, rivers, and lakes and filled them with life. And He created you, woman.

The Bible says that we were created in the Image of God in his likeness. **Genesis 1:27 (KJV)** *"So God created man in his own image, in the image of God created him; male and female created he them."* If you're created in the likeness and image of God, Almighty, you're extremely creative and can do all things through Christ who strengthens you. So stop saying "I can't" and start saying "I can." Better yourself and make a difference in someone else's life. If God can, you're made in his image, so you can too. He has given you the power and the anointing to be used for his Glory.

Possess the power of God. He has given you the power and authority over the earth and over all evil, learn to use it. The Holy Spirit or Holy Ghost gives us the power to take back whatever the devil has taken from us, but before he can take it, you can stop him. What I love about the power of the anointing is it grows to different levels. At each level, you become stronger, wiser and fearless. There's no devil in hell that can hold you down nor stop you from becoming the woman of God you were called to be. I can do all things through Christ who strengthens me.

Worksheet #3

I can do all things through Christ. Phil. 4:13

QUESTION: What are some interests you may have and desires to accomplish in life? What are you waiting for? Start working on them now. List your goals.

1. _____

2. _____

3. _____

4. _____

5. _____

6. _____

7. _____

8. _____

9. _____

10. _____

SUMMARY

You were created in the image of God, the author, and creator of everything. You have the ability to create and to do anything that you set your mind to do.

PRAYER

Father, God, we come to you through our Lord and Savior, Jesus Christ. I want my desires to be your desires. Help me to see that I can do all things with the strength you give to me. I ask that you give to me the will to set and accomplish my goals in life so that I can be all that I need to be to serve out my purpose in the Kingdom of God. Amen.

Step 4 - Speak Favor Over Your Finances.

2 Peter 1:4 (KJV)

Whereby are given unto us exceeding great and precious promises: that by these ye might be partakers of the divine nature, having escaped the corruption that is in the world through lust.

As Christian women we should not be living in financial poverty, remember we are royalty, joint-heir to Christ, but things do happen. As single women, we sometimes get weary when its comes to our finances, especially if we have children. Those without children sometimes have it harder. When you're in a financial bind, there is no assistance from any agency because you have no children.

God doesn't want us to worry and be anxious for anything. It is his desires for us to be prosperous in all

35

that we do. For some of us, we live paycheck to paycheck, and robbing Peter to pay Paul only puts us in a deeper hole. For parents, we tend to put our children's needs above our own, so we go without, then when payday comes around, and the bills are paid, you're left with $47 for the next two weeks. You're trying to decide if you should buy the toilet paper or put gas in the car to get to work and you still need food for the house.

Now is the time to pray and ask God to help you find yourself and to give him all your worries and fears. The worst thing you can get caught up in is early paydays. These little establishments are designed to keep you in debt to them. You only went there because you had no money and now you're in more debt to someone else. Seriously, if you want a financial breakthrough, you have to let go of your independence and surrender it all to God. God will show you favor and open up doors you never thought would open. Even in your lack, God will always make a way if you just trust the process. God can cancel all of your debt, I know this to be a fact.

Be good stewards over your finances. The Bible says in Luke 12:42 (KJV), *" Who then is that faithful and wise steward whom his lord shall make ruler over his household to give them their portion of meat in due season."* Throughout the word of God, he refers to a good steward as being trustworthy.

If God can trust us with our expenses, he will bless us with greater and makes us rulers of many. For a lot of us, living in lack has become a normal thing because we grew up with lack. Learn to break that generational curse of poverty and lack. God has given us the power to cast down evil spirits and no weapon formed against you will prosper. If Satan can keep you in bondage, wrapped up in poverty, then he has access to your life and your home. Take back what belongs to you,

Jesus said in his word, "I have come that you might have life and have it more abundantly; it's a choice how you decide to live. Change your mindset, change your life. Speak increase in your life spiritually and financially.

Lisa Moore-Banks

The world is going to shambles and who knows where the economy will end up when it's all said and done by 2020. But we, as Christians, must remain steadfast, unmovable and hold onto the promises of God; he is our only source of help.

Worksheet #4

Pray over your finances every payday before you spend.

- Keep record of your bank account
- Pay 10% tithes
- Put minimum of $50 into savings every payday
- Pay all your bills on time (helps build up credit score)
- Spend wisely, buy what you need and less of what you want
- Pay yourself a minimum of 5% of you check each pay
- Keep a log and receipts of all your expenses
- Invest into one small credit card to help build up your credit score
- Seek financial counseling for help
- Do NOT go to any early payday loan companies they will keep you in debt

NOTE: Best to consult with a financial advisor or your bank for the best plan for you.

Budget Expenses, miscellaneous and wants; Monthly, Biweekly or Weekly

Lisa Moore-Banks

Net Amount: **1st Pay** $_____
TITHES $_____

Expenses:
   1. **Rent/Mortgage**
                          $_____
   2. **Utilities**
                          $_____
   3. **Car**
                          $_____
   4. **Insurance**
                          $_____
   5. **Food**
                          $_____
   6. Daycare
                          $_____
   7. Miscellaneous
                          $_____
   8. Needs
                          $_____

TOTAL $_____
ADD TITHES AMOUNT $_____

     TOTAL EXPENSES $_____

**TOTAL EXPENSES SUBTRACT FROM NET
INCOME = $_____**

ADD REMAINDER TO YOUR SAVINGS ACCOUNT.

SUMMARY

God sees and knows all about your financial difficulties. Trust God for everything that you need. You must give it to him by releasing your faith. Believe he is your provider. If the rent is due, know in your heart and seek God for favor. Even if you never receive money in your hands, God will give grace and favor over the situation. God will and can cancel all your debt and work miracles in your finances. Although the nation's economy is hit, getting worse by the day, this does not mean your finances will be. God has a much bigger plan for his people, that we will stand out from among them and be a prosperous people, all for the glory of God.

Be a good steward.

PRAYER

Lisa Moore-Banks

Father, God, we come boldly to the throne of grace seeking your face. Lord, please forgive us for not being good stewards over our finances. I ask that you find favor and help me to understand and give me wisdom over my finances. I ask that you find mercy upon me and cancel any and ALL debt in the mighty name of Jesus Christ. Amen.

Step 5 - Let's Talk About Sex Ladies.

I Corinthians 6:18 (KJV)
Flee fornication, every sin that a man doeth is without the body but that committeth fornication sinneth against his own body.

I want to address the elephant that's always in the room at most Bible studies discussing how to deal with a single woman's sexual desires. I say this because most single Christian women are afraid to discuss the feelings they have about sexual needs and how to handle their sexual desires.

Going without answers to the questions in your mind creates a lack of knowledge and understanding. Therefore, you can't receive the wisdom to handle desires and end up in bed with "June bug" from way back when. We are only human, and women were

43

created for men. God designed us for the reproduction of this world. So, it's in our DNA, in our flesh, it's a part of nature.

The act of having sex is not a sin, but not being legally (married) to have sex is a sin against God's word and it's not of God. You must be married, joined by God, and not going around having intercourse trying to fulfill your fleshly desires. Ladies, remaining a virgin until marriage for both men and women is so important; only two spirits that are of God will join as one. The more men you have sex with, the more spirits you have allowed within you. There is no telling how many women he has already slept with, and the Holy Spirit cannot dwell in an unclean temple.

For most of us single, saved women, we were sexually active before repentance and, as a born again Christian, we are now practicing celibacy. For those of you who are still virgins, congratulations and be proud and continue to hold on to your most prized possession. Your future husband will love and respect you even more. Your virginity is very rare and precious. I'm sure there is a struggle to maintain your innocence, but do not give in to temptation from the devil. God is powerful, and he can keep you.

But what about the rest of us who once were sexually active or addicted to sex? There's a big difference, and you're going to want to take notes because I have a word for you.

This step will help you understand why you have sexual desires in the middle of the night. Why sometimes it feels as though someone is on top of you or your back when lying in bed. Understand the reason why you wake up in the morning feeling as though you had sex all night long. Although you are never physically having sex, you're left feeling emotional and unworthy of God's love. Reason being, "night demons" named Incubus and Succubus. They are known as sex demons of the night. Merriam-Webster.com defines these demons as:

☐ **Incubus (male sex demon):** An evil spirit that lies on a person (usually on a female) in her sleep and has sexual intercourse with her while sleeping.

How do I know when Incubus has visited me?

A. At night when you're asleep overwhelming urge to have sex

B. Feeling of heaviness on top of you or in back of you when in bed

C. Vivid dreams of having sexual intercourse

D. Orgasmic feelings while in your sleep or waking up

E. Masturbation

F. Overwhelmed with guilt and fear afterward

NOTE: Masturbation is never mentioned in the Bible or made known as a sin. However, sexual immorality and lasciviousness is a sin against God's word. Performing this lustful act takes your mind and attention away from God and results in disconnecting your relationship with him. Remember the Holy Spirit cannot dwell in an unclean temple. This allows any evil spirit to enter in, causing you to do some crazy, explicit sexual things, leaving you feeling unworthy of anything, especially forgiveness and the love of God.

However, you can be forgiven and still and always will be loved by God. God hates the sin, but will always love you. However, he will not tolerate anyone willfully sinning against his word.

☐ **Succubus (female sex demon):** defined as a female demon who overpowers men to have sexual intercourse with her in their sleep.

NOTE: This demon attacks the men in the same way as Incubus attack the women.

What brings these demons into our beds in the middle of the night? Our lustful desires to have sex. You may think you do not desire to have a sexual encounter, but deep down the feelings are there. If there's any disconnection with God, this will cause any evil spirit to enter into your life. If you're recovering from sexual addictions, you are the one incubus seeks after the most.

These sexual demons are very powerful and will take complete control over you if you don't fight back and go into spiritual warfare. God has given us the power to fight back and win this battle. It's up to us to stay in prayer and fast, submitting our bodies as a living sacrifice unto Jesus Christ and feed our souls with the Word of God. Doing this will keep your mind off anything that's not of God.

Do you ever get strong orgasmic urges to have sex during that time of the month or right before or after? This is the work of Incubus trying to control you. It's just another way for Satan to get into your life and pull you out of the will of God. If you are overpowered, fight with the word of God, and the devil will flee.

Being single does not mean something is wrong. You are beautiful, fearfully and wonderfully made by God. Learn to make dates with other female friends who are single, or take yourself out on a date. When the right person comes along, and your relationship with God is on point, you will know if he's the one to date or to marry. God will never leave you nor forsake you in any part of your life because he is your life. Think of celibacy, not as a punishment, but look at it as total surrendering unto God.

Paul says in *I Corinthians 7:7-8 "For I would rather all men were even as I myself (single). But every man hath proper gift from God, one after this manner, and another after that. 8-I say therefore to the unmarried and widows; It is good for them if they abide even as I.*

Being alone can be a good thing in this season of your life. This gives you a chance to establish a real relationship with God. The closer you are to his heart, the more you will fall head over heels in love with Christ. A real man of God should be able to see the love of God in your heart and see Jesus Christ's light shine within you. That will draw him to you. Until then, God will meet every need.

Go ahead, ask the Lord for a Hug. I have experienced this, and it's amazing and more satisfying than having sex. Learn to get intimate with God.

Worksheet #5

Take your focus away from not having a man in your life. Make a list of what you're doing or not doing to stay focused on God.

Things I am doing:

1. _____

2. _____

3. _____

4. _____

5. _____

Things I need to do:

1. _____

2. _____

3. _____

4. _____

5. _____

SUMMARY

Having a healthy sexual relationship is perfectly normal and God has created and designed our bodies to engage in the act of making love. However, there are commandments from God not to have sex while single, so if you're committing fornication, this is a sin. Participating in sexual activities alone, masturbating, although it's never mentioned in the bible, doesn't mean it's ok with God, there are major consequences for this lustful act.

Beware of your thoughts of having sexual activities; "you think long, you think wrong." Entertaining the thought will then send Satan signals to send powerful sexual night demons into your life. BUT God! Our God is Stronger. Our God Is Bigger! Put on the whole armor of God so that you can withstand the wiles of the enemy. Know that God understands your concerns for not having a husband.

If your desires are to be married, hold onto your faith that you will become "Mrs. Somebody."

Begin to ask God how to prepare for your husband to be. What can you do as a saved woman of God to get ready for your Boaz and stop obsessing about having a husband and focus all your attention on God?

PRAYER

Father God, I come to you through your son my Lord and Savior, Jesus Christ. Lord help me to have self-control over my sexual desires, let my desires be your desires for me to wait and not sin against your word. Lord shield me at night while I sleep from sex demons that want to lead me astray. I vow to wait on you, Lord, to send my husband, who was created just for me so that I might not sin against your word. Amen.

Step 6 - Develop a Lifestyle of Prayer, Praise, and Worship.

I Thessalonians 5:17 (KJV)

Pray without ceasing.

Prayer and worship are our only connection to God. The only way to hear him, see him and feel him is through prayer, praise, and worship. However, there's a difference in having a prayer life and a life of praise and worship. All can be done orally or mentally in your mind from within the heart. For the best results, it's always good to open up your mouth and praise the Lord and worship God in Spirit and Truth. John 4:24 (KJV)

- **Prayer:** **A conversation with God**
- **Praise:** **Expression of gratitude of thanks**
- **Worship:** **To have intense love and admiration, to be in awe**

Lisa Moore-Banks

How: A heart that is -

- Earnest
- Humble
- Sincere
- Desire
- Admiration
- Love

When: Constantly all day every day -

- Morning
- Afternoon
- Evening
- Night

Where: Anywhere, any time of the day within your heart -

- Store
- Car
- Work
- Church
- Restroom
- Shower

- Walking

Action: Movement any way you can -

- Speaking
- Singing
- Clapping of hands
- Lifting of hands
- Dancing
- Waving of Flags

Worship

There is no other way to worship God than in spirit and truth. Your heart, mind, and soul must be in the right condition to receive his presence. What I mean by conditions; there should be no other thoughts but of God. There should be no sin in your heart. Your soul must line up with God's spirit. There should always be a relationship with God in order to worship him and to develop a relationship. You must stay connected to him.

SUMMARY

God loves to be connected to his people in prayer, praise, and worship; after all, we are created to be a praise for his glory. When we praise God in worship, it releases blessings and breakthroughs. When you're in constant prayer and praise, it doesn't allow room for the devil to cause chaos in your life. Be consistent in prayer, praise, and worship. It's our 911 emergency line and our 411 information line to the Holy Ghost. However, we must spiritually dial up the operator, Jesus Christ, to get all calls through.

NOTE: Pastor Kim Lyons has a prayer line each month at 6 am for the first seven days of the month. PRAYER IMPACT (641) 715-3670 Access Code 411599# After you enter the code, push mute, then just listen to her anointed prayer and pray in agreement. You will be blessed!

PRAYER

Father, God, I ask that you give me the spirit of boldness to learn how to pray. I know this is my only way to get connected to you to have an intimate relationship as I worship your Holy name. Help me to pray fervently and to pray for others. Amen.

Lisa Moore-Banks

Worksheet #6

~Write a Love Letter to God in Prayer.

_____

_____

_____

_____

_____

_____

_____

_____

_____

_____

_____

_____

_____

_____

_____

_____

_____

Amen.

Step 7 - Change Your Mindset Change Your Life.

Romans 12:2 (KJV)

Be not conformed to this world, but be ye transformed by the renewing of your mind, that you may prove what is that good and acceptable, perfect will of God.

The way you see yourself reflects on how you look at life. How you live your life can reflect the outcome of how you view your purpose in the Kingdom of God. Your mindset plays a great part on where you are in life and where you're going in your future. If you're a woman with low self-esteem, always putting yourself down and do not value what God has put in you, then you have lowered your standards in life and your purpose for the Kingdom of God.

You're no longer the woman who use to be
"_____," whatever you did before repentance.
You're not the whoremonger, always having sex with
the first man who comes your way. You're not the
drunk in the club partying until morning light. You're
not the mother who neglects her children. You're not
the woman who lives in poverty or lack, who can't
keep up with bills and who is always receiving an
eviction notice. You're not the woman who is bitter
and depressed. You are NOT that woman anymore;
you are a child of the Most High God, joint-heir with
The King of Kings, Jesus Christ.

The world lives in lack because they do not have
the same spiritual DNA as we do; DNA that connects
you to Jesus Christ. There is nothing God cannot do,
even in the worse times of your life, he was already
there. But, it's our mindset that keeps us from
believing that he can and he will. We allow self to get
in the way of our blessings because of our mindset
that creates self-doubt. If you know that God woke
you up this morning, why not know that he can heal
you, or get that loan for your new car? You have to
know that you know who you are.

Although you may not have money in your bank account or lost your job and the balance says $0, know that God will take care of you. The job you've been wanting, claim it as yours. The house you ride by and look at, claim it as yours. It all belongs to your Father, God, in Heaven, and what belongs to him, belongs to you and me. But, you have to change your mindset to change your life.

One of the biggest things that challenge us as single women, that stops us from changing our mindset, is the spirit of fear. Fear will cripple you and walk all over your life. Fear is a spirit with a mind of its own. If you allow fear to creep into a situation, it will completely take over and make a mess of things and cause horrific chaos. If you have a fear of approaching people, then you will never get anything done. For instance, you have a bill that is due, you know you do not have the money, and you are in disconnect, the challenge is calling to see if you can get an extension on the due date until your next payday. However, fear creeps in, and you are overwhelmed with the terror of talking to someone to ask for help. Remember the person on the other line has no control over you.

This happens because of our mindset. Perhaps you were in an abusive environment, or just low self-esteem prevents you from having boldness and confidence. Even if they do say no, remember God is in control and has a plan already set in motion to work it all out. With God, all things are possible. Asking for God to give you the spirit of BOLDNESS is changing your mindset. Then sit back and watch things begin to change.

You're probably thinking, how do you begin to change your mindset? Start with an attitude adjustment. You cannot be a negative person and expect your mindset to change. You must change your way of thinking, and you must watch what you speak into the atmosphere. If you're going to keep saying, "I'm broke," then you will be broke. Stop saying "I'm tired" when it's time to do anything or go anywhere. The number one thing to leave out of your vocabulary is the word "can't." Change it to "I can do all things through Christ who strengthens me." But all this won't matter if you don't change your heart. It has to get deep down into your heart, and you must believe that you are an overcomer, you are successful, you have the Spirit of God within you to do all that he has called you to do because you are a joint heir with Jesus Christ.

Repeat after me, *"I AM BLESSED AND HIGHLY FAVORED BY GOD."* I want you to look in the mirror and tell yourself that every day, and when someone asks you, "how are you doing," that is how you are to reply. Watch God change your mindset and your attitude.

A Few Scripture to Help With Mindset

Galatians 5:22-23: Fruit of The Spirit

Proverbs 31:10-31: Proverb 31 Woman

Psalms 19:14: Let The Words of My Mouth

Psalms 23: Lord is My Shepherd

Psalms 37: Fret Not Thyself of evildoers (Don't worry)

Psalms 34: Bless the Lord All Times

Ephesians 6:10-18: Put on the Whole Armor

John 3:16: God Loves You

Worksheet #7

Attitude Adjustment.

"What can I do to change my way of thinking negative into a positive mindset?" After listing your goals complete each goal in a time frame of 180 days. After six months, it becomes a habit.

Positive Mindset Goals

1. _____

2. _____

3. _____

4. _____

5. _____

6. _____

7. _____

8. _____

9. _____

SUMMARY

You are blessed and highly favored by God. You are a joint heir with Jesus Christ. If you can believe this within your heart, you have taken the first step to changing your mindset. Having a negative attitude only brings the wrong things into your life. Keeping your mind set on Jesus Christ will only bring good things into your life.

PRAYER

Father, in the name of Jesus Christ, help me to always think on good things and to keep my mind set on you and not this world. Amen.

Lisa Moore-Banks

Step 8 - Forgive Yourself and Others.

II Corinthians 5:17 (KJV)
Therefore if any man be in Christ he is a new creature, old things have passed away, behold all things are become new.

The power of forgiveness can change your life. Holding on to past hurts or what someone has said or done to you over 5, 10, 15, or 20 years ago can literally destroy you. Being angry over the things that you cannot change will only create bitterness and depression and in some cases illness or death.

You simply cannot hold onto things that don't edify your heart, mind, body and soul. In doing so, this allows the devil to feed off the negativity and create events of chaos into your life.

Do you always seem to be struggling in some way? Not being able to find happiness, even in the littlest things that should make you smile. Some people are so angry and bitter that when they see a cute baby cooing with joy, they find it hard to crack a smile; or when your best friend announces her engagement, you can't even be happy for her because you're to busy carrying bitterness in your heart. You have created a shield, a wall around your heart refusing to let the divine love of God enter.

Why is this? Forgive your past. Why can't you let go? Because you don't feel worthy of being loved due to the things you have done or what someone has done to you in your past before repentance. You have to forgive yourself and them.

If you are still holding on to your guilt and shame, *right now in the Name Of Jesus Christ, I command Satan to release you of his trickery from the demonic spirits of guilt and shame! Amen!*

Now since you have come to repentance, did you know that God does NOT even remember what you have done, so why should you? So, why continue to ask God for forgiveness for things that he doesn't remember that you have done? God has cast all your sins and the old you into the sea of forgetfulness (Micah 7:19) and he remembers them no more. He forgave us from what we think is the worse things ever and some have done worse than others, but with God, he doesn't compare our sins to be greater or lesser than others, and he forgives us all the same.

Quoting my friend, *Mother Gladys English*, *"God is not a third party person, he doesn't take sides or choose to be on one side or the other when it comes to us, he only cares about two sides, that is right & wrong."* God is a good, loving God who loves us all unconditionally. He will always love us for who we are. You are a new creature in Christ, you have been transformed in the beauty of holiness in Jesus Christ. You are no longer a sinner, of adultery and fornication, a streetwalker of the night, a drunk in the club, a deadbeat mama or a thief. You have been forgiven and given another life, filled with new mercies and grace daily.

This is your opportunity to take advantage of the new you and be who God has purposed you to be.

Worksheet #8

Forgiveness is unlocking the door to set someone free and realizing you were the prisoner. - Unknown

Write on a separate sheet of paper and list the things that you hold in your heart for which you have not forgiven yourself or others; then say the prayer below and shred the sheet of paper. After you have done this, immediately throw it outside in the trash, get it out of your home and remember it no more.

Prayer for the Releasing of Unforgiveness:

Father, God, I thank you for your forgiving power and love. Thank you for new mercies and grace daily, so if I fall, I can quickly rise to worship you in spirit and truth with the anointing power of the Holy Ghost. Satan, I come against you in the name of Jesus Christ. I command you to release me from the spirit of guilt and shame that keeps my heart from forgiving myself and others.

Satan, I am NO longer a prisoner of unforgiveness! You are a liar from the pits of hell! You have no power and you have no authority over me! God said in his word, in Micah 7:19, I AM FORGIVEN, AND HE DOES NOT REMEMBER IT ANYMORE! I refuse to allow you to bring it back to my remembrance so that I can walk in my purpose to fulfill my calling for the Kingdom of God.

Father, God, I trust and believe that I have been released and the shield of unforgiveness has been broken from my heart. I believe that you are now pouring your divine love into my heart and I am free. In the name of the Father and the Son and the Holy Ghost. AMEN!

Shout, "HALLELUJAH, TO GOD BE THE GLORY, I'M FREE!"

SUMMARY

Always keep prayers of forgiveness in your heart daily, forgiving others and yourself. Keep a prayer of repentance in your heart always. Cast down the thoughts of sin that Satan tries to make you remember. You have power and authority over him. He has absolutely none over you. If you feel that you are not this person, think again. God knows what is really in your heart and my advice to you is to say the prayer to save yourself.

PRAYER

Father, God, we thank you for forgiving us of all our sins. We thank you for the power to forgive others and ourselves. Lord, create in me a pure and clean heart that I might not sin against you.

If I should fall, thank you for new mercy and grace that follows me all the days of my life. Lord, I love you and will forever be grateful, in Jesus Name. Amen.

Step 9 - Learn To Be Submissive.

Titus 3:2 (KJV)
To speak evil of no one, to be no brawlers, but gentle showing all meekness unto all men.

Submissive - ready to conform to the authority or the will of others; meekly obedient or passive.

Well, ladies, you are now three steps away from walking into your purpose. I trust that you are getting a better understanding of how to get started and yield to the calling of Jesus Christ for the Kingdom of God. If not, you still have three more lessons, and I'm pretty sure that you will soon catch on and start piecing it all together and it will make sense. Besides, I still have a lot more to cover before you even start thinking about your journey into your purpose, if you haven't already done so. To get started, you have to learn to become submissive unto God's will and his way.

I have given you the definition of submissive. When being submissive, you cannot have an attitude or question God. You possess and take ownership of the Fruit of the Spirit; the one that stands out and is needed for your ungodly attitude is "meekness."

A meek woman of God is quiet, gentle and easily imposed on; meaning you don't have to argue with her to get her to do anything that's within reason. On the spiritual side of things, we are willing vessels unto God. This can truly be a challenge because most singles have the tendency to be "Lil Miss Independent," and "I can do things my way and I don't need any help." We will get offended if you think you can take over and tell us how to do things or that we may need to change what we have created for our family or ourselves. Need I say more... "Change your mindset"... exactly.

We allow our independence to get in the way of God's plans for our life. If we don't like how things are going, we then turn around and fix it ourselves, when a God delay is our answer to prayer. We don't realize that we are blocking blessings and stunting our growth by not being submissive to God's will. You can't be submissive with a capital "I."

When things are going right, and all is well, we tend to use the word "I" a lot. "I did this," "I did that," when you should be saying "look what God has done for me," "God did it for me." Like the scripture says, "I can do all things through Christ." It's only by the grace of God you were able to do anything that you have accomplished or avoided in life. It was all his will and not of your own.

It's very important to be submissive, willing and ready to listen to his voice and willing to answer to his call without grumbling or complaining. When you are asked, be ready to speak or to work in the church. Now that you have learned to be submissive to God and the church, you can serve without having something negative to say and be joyful and happy about serving out the will of God. This all plays a bigger part into God's plans and purpose for your life, especially if you are planning to get married one day. God is preparing you to become a submissive wife, who is clothed in meekness, free from complaining, grumbling, and arguing. You are willing and happy to serve your man. Happy wife means a happy life, all because you have learned to become submissive to God and the Church.

So possess the Fruit of the Spirit, not just meekness but all nine of them. Simpler terms, just be obedient in doing the will of God and making him your priority in life. Fully and totally surrendering your life to Christ will enable you to live a submissive life to God.

How do you learn to become submissive unto the Lord? With you heart, mind, body and soul. Give God your all through fasting. Fasting means to abstain from food or drink or both. Making this sacrifice to God signifies you're willing to give up what's important to you and your body because you want more of him. This will help discipline you and help you to become more submissive to God. Being submissive means that you must give him all of you. So, I encourage you to fast as the scripture says In **I Corinthians 7:5**, *Defraud ye not one the other, except [it be] with consent for a time, that ye may give yourselves to fasting and prayer; and come* *together again, that Satan tempt you not for your incontinency.*

If you don't know when to fast or how to fast, seek the Lord about this or ask your Pastor. Some churches announce a fast but fasting should also be personal, as well. I usually fast three times a week: Sunday, Tues, and Thurs from midnight the night before until three in the afternoon. These are the days I go to church.

There are many different types and different methods of fasting, such as the Daniel Fast, but always research and seek God. Fasting is merely giving up temporarily the things you are accustomed to such as social media, for a time; for we know that these things can be a distraction to our time with the Lord.

When fasting, be prepared for Satan to distract you and tempt you to get off your fast. He did it to Jesus, and he will do it to you. Cast him down back to the pit of Hell! And if you should fail, as I have many times, don't feel bad because God honors your heart and he gives you the grace to try again. Fasting helps you to develop into the woman of God you are purposed to be.

Worksheet #9

Meekness is power that is totally and completely surrendered to God's control. – Unknown.

True or False
Submissive women are strong willed
- ☐ True
- ☐ False

Meekness is a Fruit of the Spirit
- ☐ True
- ☐ False

There are 8 Fruits of the Spirit
- ☐ True
- ☐ False

A woman who is submissive is fearfully & wonderfully made
- ☐ True
- ☐ False

Abstaining from the things you love most such as food, drink, and social media is a form of submission?

☐ True
☐ False

SUMMARY

The nature of a good, virtuous woman possesses the Fruits of the Spirit; she is clothed in meekness and shall inherit the earth. Being submissive does not mean you are a weak woman, in fact, you're strong and mighty. Being obedient to God's will and his ways is being a woman who is willing to be submissive to the Lord. If you can be submissive to God and the Church, you will become a woman of virtue, and that's what will attract the man of God who may be your potential husband. Know that fasting is a way to become totally submissive unto God, seek the Lord on ways and methods of doing so.

PRAYER

Father, God, thank you for new mercies and grace. Lord, I seek to do your will and to be humble and submissive to you, putting your desire above my desires. Help me to live and walk in all 9 of the Fruits of the Spirit, in Jesus Name. Amen.

Answers to True or False:

1. False- We are not to be strong willed of our own, only when following the will of God

2. True-   Fruits of the Spirit, Galatians 5:22-23

3. False- There are nine fruits of the spirits, see Galatians 5:22-23

4. **True-**   Psalms 139:14

5. True- Fasting is a method of submission unto God.

Step 10 - Be Consistent

I Corinthians 15:58 (KJV)
Therefore my beloved brethren be ye steadfast unmovable always abounding in the work of the Lord, forasmuch as ye know that your labour is not in vain in the Lord.

In your journey with Jesus Christ, you must learn to stay consistent in your walk of faith and stay faithful to God. Going to Bible study on weeknights or Sunday morning service are good ways to feed your spirit man, however, be consistent in your prayer life and your praise and worship.

Seek after God daily, applying the word of God in your life 24/7. Yes, it's possible to praise God even in your sleep. It has been many times that I have rolled over with a 'thank you, Jesus" coming from my mouth or a sweet melody of praise.

Now that you're learning and growing, the enemy will begin to attack you from the left and right. Don't be afraid to fight back! You are now walking with your two new best friends, Wisdom and Knowledge. You're now on the top of Satan's list of priorities to stop you, block you, and drop you down on the ground; but he can't.

In the growth process, you're beginning to realize exactly who you are in Jesus Christ, and Satan has fought you tooth and nail to keep you from getting to know who you are and what you're really capable of in the Kingdom of God. Not being faithful and consistent keeps your blessings on lockdown, but being faithful in prayer, praise and worship releases the power within you for your calling and anointing.

When desiring to be consistent, there is no room to waver. When you find yourself up one day, and down the next day, this makes room for Satan to come in for the attack. It is very important to feed your soul with the bread of life every day and to assemble yourselves with one another and be part of a ministry that is on fire for Jesus Christ. Put yourself under the leadership of pastors who care for the people of God enough to reveal themselves and their past sins. Leaders who love the Lord so much that they preach/teach straight out of the word of God, with no sugar coating or removal of the word, just "REAL TALK" on the real word. This type of teaching is rare and will help you to enjoy coming to church to hear the word of God, desiring to seek after him all the more.

Stabilize yourself in one place. You can't be a church hopper going from church to church. People who can't sit still at one church are usually people who have issues within themselves. If you are always finding fault in others and leave the church and the next church and the next, guess what? It's really you. You're taking yourself everywhere you go with the same issues you had at the first church. You need to be delivered and set free. Stop running from whatever it is that God is trying to get through to you.

Don't allow Satan to come in and steal, kill and destroy you. God is trying to develop you and grow you up for positioning, to place you in your calling. Not everything is Satan's fault. Sometimes God allows things to happen so we can grow up and stop whining and crying about the same problems and issues. Quit being "spiritually spoiled," expecting every need to be met without putting in any effort to do the will of God. He doesn't have to hand over everything on a silver platter.

Everything does happen for a reason, so magnify God and give him glory and praise. Whatever is happening now, good or bad in your life, was all created and designed by God, purposed for you to go through and overcome so that it can be a part of your ministry. So continue to stay focused and faithful. Consistently resist the devil, and he will flee. It was never about you; it was always for the Glory of God and for the benefit of helping you to become a woman of God with purpose. Being purposed to do the will of God is the best way to stay consistent.

Worksheet #10

List some ways that will help you have a consistent state of mind to remain faithful to God.

1_____

2_____

3_____

SUMMARY

No matter what comes or goes in your life, whatever the issues or situation may be, remain consistent in your relationship with the Lord. Continue to lift up his name in praise and worship. Being consistent will increase your faith, and God will see that you are really trying to get closer to him. However, be prepared for him to allow some sort of problem to arise to test your faith in him. The only way you can pass the test is to remain consistent and not waver. Stay in the word, stay on your knees, and turn your plate away in fasting. Always give God the praise for everything, the good the bad and the ugly problems or chaotic situations in your life. You are a strong and courageous woman of God, and nothing can stop you, nor block you, from what God has called you to be.

PRAYER

Father, God, help me to become steadfast and unmovable in my daily walk with you. I desire to be consistent in all that I do for your will and your glory. I will delight myself unto you always and forever. Amen.

Step 11 - The Spiritual Birthing of Your Purpose.

I John 5:4 (KJV)
For whatsoever is born of God overcometh the world: and this is the victory that overcometh the world, even our faith.

If you are reading this book, I believe in my spirit, you are purposed to have this handbook for the very reason that God has a calling on your life, and the Lord is about to do some extraordinary things for some ordinary, single women of God. In this season of your life, you will begin to experience the fullness of God. God will begin to show you a vision if you have not already seen his Glory manifested through you. Also, with this season comes a purge. God will start removing everything that will cause hindrance. God will block people and remove people out of your life. These are people who are negative and critical of you and don't believe in you. God doesn't want any distraction that may interfere with the work he's about to do in you. Everyone won't be a part of what God has for you simply because they are not at the level to receive you. When the season has come, they shall return unto you and see the glory of God's love, peace, and truth within you, says the Lord.

The vision is God's plan for your life, and for you to receive the vision, you have to be in the right conditions for God to position you for his purpose. What God put in you must go through birthing stages; this is how you grow into the position to which you have been called.

From the first day of repentance until the first day of walking in your calling; whether it be evangelizing, pastoring, teaching, preaching or mentoring, whatever God has called you to do, your purpose is similar to being pregnant. Birthing out your calling is like going through each stage of pregnancy called trimesters, then there is labor and delivery.

Trimester I

➢ *Transformation Stage*- You are now changing physically and spiritually. You are no longer the woman you use to be from the inside out. You have a glow about you; the anointing is hovering over you. The spiritual morning sickness comes from not knowing exactly where you fit in or what's really going on inside you. This leaves you feeling emotional and confused because it's all new to you.

Trimester II

➢ *Movement Stage-* The power of the anointing of the Holy Ghost is moving within you. You're finding a place of comfort within the church. Now you are experiencing growth and development by regularly attending weekly services and prayer. You're getting to know God and feel his presence around you. You feel good and comfortable out shopping for new Cds and DVDs. You're always craving and eating the word of God, hungry for the Lord. You are no longer having morning sickness. You know where you belong, not of the world, you're just happy in the Lord because you have found out who you are in Christ.

Trimester III

> *Uncomfortable Stage*- Although you are still happy and excited about your relationship with Christ, your life is getting tight and extremely uncomfortable. The devil knows it's your time; you are due soon for the delivery of your calling and purpose for the Kingdom of God. You don't feel prepared and ready. You worry about the littlest things. You feel disconnected from Jesus, although you have been married for a while now, because you feel miserable and unworthy. You think you're ready, but it's all in God's timing. Count it all Joy.

The Labor Process

> **Discomfort and Pain Stage**- Just like labor pains come every 5 to 15 mins and get closer and closer, so does the trials and tribulations. They keep hitting you, back to back, each one gets harder and harder. Sometimes you have thoughts of why did I even think I could do this? You question God's way of delivery. You can't handle the pain and you want to have a natural way of God's commandments. Your attitude has changed to become mean and hateful because laboring is so hard, you just want the easy way out. But you must walk through the valley of the shadow of death and fear no evil, for The Lord is with you. You are strong in the Lord; he has given you the back to P.U.S.H hard; Pray Until Something Happens.

. **The Delivery**

> *The Arrival*- It's over now. You are beautiful, spiritually healthy and strong. You

finally got your breakthrough; you are now in the purpose in which God has called you. You can handle anything that comes your way, you have tough skin and nothing can break you.

The spiritual birthing process prepares you for your calling. Everything you have gone through in life was designed and purposed by God for this moment, right here, in your life. You know God has a calling on your life, he's about to unleash a special anointing on you and place you in position so that you can do the will of the Lord.

You are a true soldier in the army of the Lord, and you are equipped to fight with power and authority and no fear. You are now living in perfect peace. Accept this word from our God and possess it.

Worksheet #11

Mold me, make me.

Write down the vision that God has given to you for your life:

_____

_____

_____

_____

_____

_____

_____

_____

_____

_____

_____

_____

_____

SUMMARY

The process for your purpose in life will at times be difficult and painful. Trials and tribulations are purposed and designed to position you into your calling for the Kingdom of God. When they say, "everything happens for a reason," this is true, and that reason being, your need to grow up and step into your purpose.

PRAYER

Father, God, I ask for forgiveness of all my sins. It's now time that I step out and receive what you have for my life. Lord, I ask that you order my steps and show me what your will for my life will be. Amen.

Step 12 - Trust God He's Faithful

Proverb 33:5-6 (KJV)
Trust in the Lord with all thine heart, and lean not to thy own understanding. In all thy ways acknowledge him and he shall direct thy path.

God has now spoken over you through this handbook written by the Holy Spirit through me as the author. However, to receive God's word that was written just for you, you must believe in him, that his word is true. To trust is to believe in something or someone 100%. While writing, I know I had to take the journey to get to this point in my life. My writing has blessed me and I have grown. I expect the same will happen for you, but you have to trust God, that he is faithful and will see you through.

Humans are visual creatures; to know that something is true or exist we must see it with our own eyes. Like with our friends, they call us "girl, I just got me a new car;" what's the first thing that comes out of our mouth? "What does it look like" or" Let me see, " or a child finds something and runs to tell the parent, they say "what is it" or "let me see." Why? Trust issues. We need to see to believe; this is why so many of us lack or haven't moved forward in our calling, we must see God to believe God. Yes, we go to church and hear a great word from the preacher, but do we really believe what they have said is the truth? Yes, we do. Why? Because we see the word of God formed in the Holy Bible, a book that we can feel by touch and see it with our own eyes. And, we see the Holy Spirit within the man or woman of God being used for his will and glory when preaching and teaching the word of God.

God is a God who can never lie or do any wrong. It's not for us to try and understand God. He may have us in the valley but it's for our good, our job is to trust him with our life and allow him to order our steps. It's not for us to understand the "whys" and "hows," we just need to know the "cans and 'wills." God can and he will. Our job is to go through it, to prove to the world that God is a:

☐ Lover- When you are lonely

☐ Healer- When you are sick

☐ Provider- When there's lack

☐ Way Maker- When there's no way

☐ My EVERYTHING I will ever need in life!

He is my life

To get to where God needs you to be, you have to trust him 100% ALL of the time and not just sometimes. Not doing so delays your progress for the process for your purpose. God loves you so much more than you can even wrap your mind around and he only wants his very best for us. Think about who God is, the miraculous creator of ALL things and the God of ALL Knowing, the Alpha and Omega. The Beginning and The End. So, why would you not trust him and his word? God's word cannot return to him void. He means what he says and says what he means. You are a strong, courageous, confident woman of God! No weapon formed against you shall prosper. You can do ALL things through Christ who strengthens you. You can't lose because you are VICTORIOUS! But you have to trust God and know that he is faithful.

There are two things that will keep you from trusting God; doubt and fear. This is not of God, it's all the work of the enemy to prevent you from reaching the destiny that God has laid out before you. Once Satan gets a whiff of the fact you are in a position to receive your calling for the purpose of the Kingdom of God, he will create doubt and fear.

Doubt comes from within the mind and plays with your thoughts. Doubt causes you to waver and be double-minded and unstable. You are not sure of anything. You want to believe it's right or wrong, true or false, but you just don't know what to believe.

Fear, on the other hand, plays with your emotions, the matter of the heart. You become afraid, so you push it away and never believe you want a part of it. You avoid it and never deal with it. This is Satan's plan to come against you and prevent you from what God has in store for you. Then you lose a hold of the vision for your calling, for the purpose of the Kingdom of God, this causes you to fall back in steps toward your destiny with Christ.

Stay focused on the Word of God and trust that he is faithful, no matter what comes or goes. God will never fail. How you handle doubt and fear may cause delays due to the fact that you must go through to get through, but God will never deny his promises. It's all purposed for the Kingdom of God. Everything that comes against you is orchestrated by God, all for the purpose for you to be able to trust in faith for the development of your spiritual growth.

Worksheet #12

Don't panic; God is with you.

Let Go and let God have his way. This is the act of total surrender and trust in his will.

Assignment: Write a list of what you are trusting God for. You are now on a higher level of anointing, so possess it like it's yours. This is the beginning of the person you were called to be in the Kingdom of God. You are a confident and courageous woman of God.

1.

2.

3.

4.

5.

6.

7.

8.

9.

Be Blessed and Be Encouraged

Woman of God, you are blessed and highly favored by God! If you know that you are saved without any doubt, then everything that appears to be wrong in your life is actually right in your life. This is all part of God's plan for your purpose.

As a Woman of God, you are strong and mighty. Be the warrior that you are in Jesus Christ. God has equipped you for each and every battle in your own personal warfare. Although it may at times appear you are losing, that is the time to seek God like never before as you are getting closer to your breakthrough and all the promises he has for your life. Remember, it was always God's will. Everything you have gone through and have done was for his glory and praise. You were created to be a praise unto him.

You have the power of the anointing of the Holy Ghost abiding within you. He will lead and guide you in the way that your life should go. Be confident and obedient in your journey with Jesus Christ; he will most definitely order each and every step toward the

Kingdom of God. Be on fire for the Lord and worship him in spirit and truth. Love the Lord, God, your Father; adore him daily. Stay in his word and feed your soul with the bread of life.

The enemy will try and turn you around, and, at times, appear bigger than yourself. However, our God is bigger, stronger and mighty than he. There is absolutely nothing God cannot do. You're never alone. Whatever you set out to do, spiritually or naturally, God has your back. The Holy Ghost has the front, and Jesus is on your left. Jesus won the war; you became victorious over 2000 years ago. What you want now from God is more power, wisdom, and knowledge to carry out the mission for Christ. Your issues were never about you. It was all created to make you who you are at this moment, today, right now, and the woman of God for all your tomorrows.

If you ever need a word of encouragement or a prayer, please feel free to send me an email. I trust that God has released a new anointing into your life. Walk in the power of God; you are created in his image so act like you know who you are; a child of the

Most High God and showing everyone the divine agape love of Jesus Christ.

Love the woman who God has created and purposed you to be. Stay positive. Get rooted deep down into the word of God to develop your strength to grow in grace. Keep the faith and conquer all evil.

So, get to stepping, woman of God! You are now *Saved Single and Satisfied* with Jesus Christ.

You are ready to walk in the purpose that you were designed and created for in the Kingdom of God. God's blessing to you my sister and friend.

Sincerely with Love,

Sis. L. Renee` Banks

Contact the Author:

EMAIL: womenofeve1@gmail.com
LINK: https://lisamoore-banks.blogspot.com

Social Media

Facebook: Lisa Moore-Banks
             Women Of E.V.E {Every Vision
             Evolves}
             Living Out Loud For Jesus Christ

Twitter: @Living4Jesus

Prayer of Repentance

Father, God, in the Name of Jesus, I do believe that Jesus Christ is the Son of God and died and rose again for all of my sins. I ask for forgiveness of all my sins, even for ones that are hidden deep within the crevices of my heart. Wash me, cleanse me and restore me to who you created me to be.

You said in your Word that if I confess with my mouth and believe in my heart, that you are Lord of Lords and risen from the grave and yet still alive, that I too can be saved and see your face in peace.

Teach me your ways, Oh Lord, help me to learn to walk right, to talk right and to live right according to the word of your commandments.

Pour out your love into my heart for others. Father, God, I thank you for your son, Jesus Christ. I believe that I am now a born again Christian, and if I get weary and worn, help me to be steadfast and unmovable.

Thank you for new grace and mercies all the days of my life. Lord, I know now that it's only You that I will ever need.

In Jesus Name. Thank God. AMEN.

TO GOD BE THE GLORY!

Lisa Moore-Banks

Made in the USA
Middletown, DE
20 February 2022